Chapter #1
The Basics of Building Habits

Have you ever wondered how some people always stay on top of things, like getting their work done on time, practicing a sport every day, or keeping their room clean? The secret isn't some magic trick—it's habits. A habit is something you do over and over again until it becomes automatic, like brushing your teeth every morning or saying "please" and "thank you." Good habits help you reach your goals and make life easier because you don't have to think about them every time you do them. They just become part of who you are.

But here's the cool part: you don't have to change everything all at once to make a difference. In fact, the best way to build a habit is to start small. Imagine you're planting a tiny seed. If you water it every day, it grows into a big tree over time. That's how habits work too. Whether you want to get better at studying, become healthier, or save money, building small habits and sticking to them can lead to big changes in your life.

This chapter is all about learning how to create good habits that help you become the best version of yourself. You'll learn how to start small, stay consistent, and use fun tricks to keep going, even when things get tough. By the end, you'll know exactly how to make good habits part of your daily routine—and you might even enjoy the process! Ready to get started on your habit-building journey? Let's go!

Small Actions Can Lead to Big Results

You might think that small actions don't make a big difference, but here's the secret: they do! Even tiny steps, when done consistently, can lead to amazing results over time. Imagine you want to get better at playing soccer.

If you practice just 10 minutes a day, those small practice sessions will add up, and before you know it, you'll be faster and better at kicking the ball.

The same is true for any habit—whether it's reading, practicing a musical instrument, or even keeping your room tidy. It's the small, daily actions that help you improve bit by bit. You don't need to make a huge change all at once.

Starting with something small, like studying for just 5 minutes a day or doing 10 jumping jacks, is enough to set you on the path to success.

Remember, small actions may not seem like much at first, but over time, they add up to big improvements!

Create a "Success Jar"! Every time you complete a small action toward your goal, write it down on a piece of paper and drop it into the jar. After a few weeks, open the jar and look at all the small actions you've taken. You'll be amazed at how much you've done!

Habits Are Like Growing Plants

Building habits is just like growing a plant—it takes time, patience, and a little bit of care every day.

When you first plant a seed, you won't see a big tree or a flower right away. But if you water the seed every day and give it sunlight, it slowly starts to grow. Over time, that small seed turns into something strong and beautiful.

Habits work the same way. When you start a new habit, like studying or practicing an instrument, you won't see big results immediately. But if you stick with it and keep doing it a little bit each day, your habit will grow stronger, and soon you'll start to see the benefits. Just like a plant needs daily attention, your habits need small, regular actions to grow.

The key is to stay patient and keep going. You might not notice the changes at first, but with time and consistency, your habit will grow just like a plant reaching toward the sun

FUN TIP

Create a "Habit Garden" on paper! For each habit, draw a plant or a flower. Every time you stick to your habit, color in a leaf or petal. Watch your habit "plant" grow stronger with each small action you take!

Focus on What You Do Every Day

It's not what you do once in a while that matters—it's what you do every day. Building good habits is all about doing small, simple actions over and over again.

Imagine trying to learn to play the piano. If you practice for 10 minutes every day, you'll improve much faster than if you practice for an hour once a month. That's because the things you do every day, even for a short time, add up and help you get better.

The same goes for other habits, like studying, exercising, or keeping your room clean. If you make a habit part of your daily routine, it becomes easier and more natural over time. The secret to building good habits is consistency—doing a little bit every day, even when you don't feel like it.

So, instead of worrying about big changes, focus on doing small actions every day. These daily efforts will make a big difference over time!

Create a "Daily Habits Calendar"! Draw or print a calendar for the month and write down one habit you want to focus on each day. For every day you complete the habit, mark it with a fun sticker or a star. Try to see how many days in a row you can keep up the habit!

Your Habits Shape Who You Are

The things you do every day—your habits—help shape the kind of person you become. If you make a habit of being helpful, you'll be known as a kind and caring person. If you make a habit of studying and learning, you'll become someone who's smart and well-prepared. Your habits are like the building blocks of your character. They show others what kind of person you are and help you become the best version of yourself.

For example, if you make it a habit to finish your homework right after school, you'll become known as someone who is responsible and reliable. On the other hand, if you get into bad habits, like ignoring chores or procrastinating, it can make life more difficult for you and others around you.

The great news is, you're in control of your habits! You get to decide what kind of person you want to be, and you can build habits that match that vision. Want to be healthier? Start exercising regularly. Want to be a better friend? Make kindness a daily habit. Over time, these actions will shape who you are.

FUN TIP

Create a "Character Poster"! On a piece of paper, draw or write down the kind of person you want to be (like "helpful," "hardworking," or "kind"). Then, list the habits that will help you become that person. Hang it up in your room to remind yourself of the habits you're building!

Build Habits that Fit the Person You Want to Be

Have you ever thought about what kind of person you want to be? Maybe you want to be a great athlete, a top student, or someone who is kind and helpful. Whatever your goal is, the habits you create today can help you become that person. Habits are like the building blocks of your future.

For example, if you want to be a better basketball player, make it a habit to practice shooting hoops for 15 minutes every day. If you want to be a better student, build a habit of doing your homework right after school. If you want to be a helpful person, try doing one kind thing for someone else every day, like helping a friend with their homework or doing a chore without being asked.

The best way to become the person you want to be is to start acting like that person now by building the right habits. Over time, these small actions will help you grow into the person you've always dreamed of being.

FUN TIP

Make a "Future You" poster! Draw a picture of what you want to be in the future—like an athlete, an artist, or a scientist. Around the picture, write down the habits that will help you get there. Hang it in your room to remind yourself of what you're working toward!

Chapter #2
How Habits Work

Have you ever noticed how some things, like brushing your teeth or tying your shoes, feel so easy that you don't even have to think about them? That's because they're habits—things you do automatically because you've done them so many times. But how do habits actually work, and why do some habits stick while others don't?

Every habit, whether good or bad, follows a simple pattern. First, there's a cue, something that reminds you to start the habit. Next, you feel a craving or desire to do the habit. Then comes the action, the habit itself, like grabbing a snack or sitting down to study. Finally, there's the reward, which is the good feeling you get after completing the habit, like feeling full after a snack or proud after finishing your homework.

Understanding this pattern helps you control your habits. If you want to build a good habit, like reading more or getting better at a sport, you can use cues and rewards to make the habit stick. And if you want to break a bad habit, like spending too much time on screens, you can change the cues that trigger it.

In this chapter, we'll learn about how habits work and how you can use that knowledge to build habits that help you reach your goals. You'll discover how small changes in your routine can make a big difference, and how understanding the pattern of habits can help you control your actions. Ready to unlock the secrets of how habits work? Let's dive in!

Every Habit Has a Pattern

Did you know that every habit you have follows the same pattern? Whether it's a good habit, like brushing your teeth, or a bad habit, like spending too much time on your phone, they all work in the same way. This pattern is made up of four parts: cue, craving, response, and reward.

- Cue: The cue is what triggers the habit. It could be something you see or feel, like walking into your room and seeing your phone, which makes you want to check it.
- Craving: This is the desire to do something. After the cue, you start to crave the action—like wanting to check your messages.
- Response: The response is the habit itself. It's the action you take, like picking up your phone and scrolling through social media.
- Reward: The reward is what you get from the habit, like feeling entertained or connected with your friends.

Understanding this pattern is really helpful because if you want to change or build a habit, you can focus on one of these steps. For example, if you want to study more, create a positive cue by leaving your books out where you can see them. If you want to break a bad habit, try removing the cue that triggers it.

FUN TIP

Turn your habits into a "Habit Detective" game! Write down the four parts (cue, craving, response, and reward) and become a detective by figuring out the pattern of your habits. Once you discover the pattern, try changing the cue or response to build a better habit!

Cues Remind You to Start a Habit

A cue is like a little reminder that tells your brain it's time to start a habit. Cues are all around you, whether you notice them or not! They can be something you see, hear, or even feel. For example, when you wake up in the morning and see your toothbrush, that's your cue to brush your teeth. Or, when you hear the school bell ring, that's your cue to get ready for class.

If you want to build a new habit, you can create your own cues to remind you. For example, if you want to practice drawing every day, leave your sketchbook on your desk where you'll see it. If you want to remember to drink more water, put a water bottle on your table so it's always in sight. When you see the cue, your brain will automatically think, "It's time to do my habit!"

On the flip side, if you want to stop a bad habit, you can try to remove the cue. For instance, if you tend to watch too much TV, try hiding the remote or putting it in a drawer.

Make "Habit Triggers"! Use sticky notes or fun drawings as cues. For example, put a sticky note on your desk that says "Study Time!" or on your water bottle with "Drink Up!" These fun, colorful cues will remind you to stick to your habit!

Cravings Are Why You Do It

A craving is what makes you want to do a habit. It's the feeling or desire you get after seeing a cue that makes you take action. For example, when you see a cookie, your craving is the desire to eat it because you know it will taste good. Or, when you see your phone, your craving might be to check messages because you're curious to see what your friends are doing.

Cravings are what drive habits. You do something because you're looking for the reward at the end, like enjoying the taste of a snack, having fun playing a video game, or feeling accomplished after finishing your homework. Understanding your cravings can help you build better habits. For example, if you crave fun, you can turn your homework into a game. If you crave a sense of accomplishment, set small goals and celebrate when you achieve them!

If you want to stop a bad habit, try changing what you crave. Instead of craving screen time, you could start craving the feeling of being productive after finishing your tasks. The key is to understand what you're craving and use it to help build habits that are good for you.

FUN TIP

Create a "Craving Switch"! If you want to change a habit, figure out what craving drives it. Then, write down a fun reward for a new, better habit. For example, if you crave fun after school, write down "Play outside for 10 minutes!" This helps you switch your craving to something positive!

The Action is the Habit

The action is the part of the habit where you actually do something. It's the behavior that happens after the cue and craving. For example, if your cue is seeing your basketball and your craving is to improve your skills, the action is practicing your basketball shots. The action is the most important part because it's the habit itself.

The more you repeat an action, the more automatic it becomes. Just like how you don't have to think much about brushing your teeth anymore—it's a habit because you've done it so many times. Actions can start out feeling like work, but the more you do them, the easier they get. Over time, they become a natural part of your day, and you don't even have to think about them.

If you want to build a new habit, focus on doing the action regularly, even if it's just for a few minutes. The more you practice, the more your brain learns to turn that action into a habit.

FUN TIP

Use the "2-Minute Rule" to help you start a habit! Commit to doing the action for just 2 minutes—whether it's reading, exercising, or practicing an instrument. After 2 minutes, you can stop or keep going. It's a fun way to make the habit feel easier!

Rewards Make You Want to Repeat the Habit

The reward is what makes you want to do a habit again and again. It's the satisfying feeling or benefit you get after completing the action. For example, after you finish your homework, the reward might be the feeling of accomplishment or free time to do something fun. Or, after eating a healthy snack, the reward might be feeling energized and strong.

Rewards are the reason habits stick. When your brain gets something positive from a habit, it remembers and wants to repeat the behavior. This is why adding a little reward to your habits can be so powerful—it keeps you motivated to keep going.

If you're building a new habit, make sure to celebrate the reward! Whether it's a high-five, a sticker on a chart, or a fun activity, rewarding yourself makes your brain feel good and encourages you to keep the habit going.

Create a "Habit Reward Jar"! Every time you complete a habit, write down a fun reward (like "watch a movie" or "play outside") and put it in the jar. At the end of the week, pick one reward from the jar to celebrate your progress!

Chapter #3
How to Build Good Habits

Have you ever wondered why some things, like brushing your teeth, feel easy, while other things, like doing homework or practicing a sport, feel harder to stick with? The difference comes down to habits. Habits are actions you do over and over again until they become automatic, like riding a bike or getting ready for bed. But here's the cool part: you can build new habits for anything you want to get better at!

Building good habits helps you reach your goals. Whether you want to improve your grades, become better at a hobby, or just stay more organized, creating positive habits makes it easier to achieve those things. Instead of trying to make one big change all at once, you start small, with actions you can do every day. Over time, these small actions build up and become a natural part of your routine.

In this chapter, we'll explore the steps to build habits that stick. You'll learn how to start small, use simple tricks to stay on track, and reward yourself for your progress. By the end, you'll have all the tools you need to create good habits that help you become the best version of yourself. Ready to learn how to make your life easier and more successful? Let's get started on building great habits!

Make Habits Easy to Start

One of the biggest secrets to building a good habit is to make it as easy as possible to get started. If a habit is easy, you're much more likely to stick with it. Imagine trying to do your homework but all your books are scattered around, or you want to practice playing the guitar, but it's tucked away in a closet. That makes it hard to get started, right?

To make habits easy, try setting things up so everything you need is ready to go. For example, if you want to practice drawing every day, keep your sketchbook and pencils on your desk so you can just grab them and start. If you want to read more, leave a book on your bed so it's the first thing you see before you go to sleep.

The easier it is to start a habit, the less you'll have to think about it. Over time, it'll become automatic, like brushing your teeth or tying your shoes!

Turn your habit into a "1-Minute Challenge!" Challenge yourself to start your habit for just one minute—whether it's reading, drawing, or doing chores. Once you start, you'll probably want to keep going, but even if you stop after a minute, you've already won by showing up!

Start with Small Habits

When it comes to building good habits, the best way to start is by thinking small. Sometimes, when you set a huge goal—like running for 30 minutes every day or reading a whole book in a week—it can feel overwhelming, and that makes it harder to stick to. Instead, start with something small and simple. Small habits are easy to do and easy to keep up with.

For example, instead of trying to run for 30 minutes, start by running for just 5 minutes each day. Want to read more? Start by reading just one page before bed. These small habits may not seem like much at first, but they're important because they're easy to stick to. And once you get used to doing small habits, you can build on them and add more over time.

The key to success is to make your habits so small that it's almost impossible to say no to doing them. That way, even on days when you don't feel like it, you can still easily manage to stick to your habit. Once you've built the small habit, you'll be surprised how quickly it grows into something bigger!

FUN TIP

Create a "Habit Streak" calendar! Each day that you do your small habit, mark an "X" on your calendar. Try to go as many days as possible without breaking your streak. Even if it's just a tiny habit, it's fun to see how long you can keep going!

Celebrate Small Wins

One of the best parts about building good habits is celebrating your progress along the way! Every time you do something positive, like sticking to a habit for a day or a week, it's important to give yourself a little reward. Celebrating small wins keeps you motivated and makes the habit-building process fun.

You don't need a big reward to celebrate. It could be something as simple as giving yourself a high-five, watching an episode of your favorite show, or taking a few extra minutes to play a game. These small celebrations make your brain feel good, and that helps your new habit stick. When your brain associates your habit with feeling good, it makes you want to do it again.

So, the next time you complete a small habit, like practicing your instrument or doing your homework, take a moment to celebrate! By recognizing your progress, you're more likely to keep going and reach even bigger goals.

FUN TIP

Create a "Victory Jar"! Every time you complete a habit, write it down on a small piece of paper and drop it into your jar. At the end of the week or month, look through all the papers to see how much progress you've made—it's like a celebration of all your hard work!

Do Habits at the Same Time Every Day

One of the easiest ways to make a habit stick is by doing it at the same time every day. When you link a habit to a specific time, it becomes part of your daily routine, just like brushing your teeth in the morning or getting dressed before school. Over time, your brain starts to expect the habit, and it becomes automatic.

For example, if you always do your homework right after school, it becomes a natural part of your after-school routine. Or, if you want to start reading more, try reading for 10 minutes before bed every night. By doing your habit at the same time, it's easier to remember and harder to forget.

It's like training your brain to expect certain activities at certain times, which helps make the habit stick. The more consistent you are, the more automatic the habit becomes. Before you know it, you won't even have to think about doing your habit—it'll just happen naturally.

FUN TIP

Set a reminder on your phone or leave a note in a place where you'll see it at the right time! If you want to practice your guitar after dinner, leave a note on the kitchen table that says, "Time to rock out!"

Connect New Habits to Old Ones

One of the easiest ways to start a new habit is by attaching it to something you already do every day. This is called habit stacking. It means you take an old habit that you already do, like brushing your teeth or having breakfast, and add a new habit right after it. This way, you don't have to remember to do the new habit—it becomes part of your routine!

For example, if you already brush your teeth every night, you could add reading a book for 10 minutes right after. Now, every time you brush your teeth, you'll remember it's time to read. Or, if you always eat breakfast in the morning, try adding a habit like practicing a hobby for 5 minutes right afterward.

By stacking your new habit onto something you already do, you won't forget to do it, and it becomes much easier to keep it going. It's like building a tower of good habits—one on top of the other!

Make a "Habit Stack Chain"! Draw a picture of each habit you want to stack, like brushing your teeth, reading, and stretching. Connect them with arrows to show how each habit leads to the next. Hang your habit chain in your room so you remember the order of your habits!

Chapter #4
Making Bad Habits Harder

We all have habits that we know aren't the best for us—whether it's spending too much time on screens, eating too many snacks, or procrastinating on homework. The tricky thing about bad habits is that they can be hard to break because they often feel easy and fun in the moment. But here's the good news: one of the best ways to stop a bad habit is by making it harder to do.

Bad habits stick around because they're often convenient or tempting. For example, if your phone is always nearby, it's easy to pick it up and scroll through social media when you're supposed to be studying. But what if you put your phone in another room while you work? By making it harder to reach, you'll be less tempted to check it. The same goes for any bad habit—if you remove the temptation or make it more difficult to do, it becomes easier to avoid.

In this chapter, we'll explore ways to make bad habits harder so they don't take over your day. You'll learn simple tricks, like creating obstacles or replacing bad habits with better ones, that will help you stay focused on your goals. Breaking bad habits doesn't have to be about willpower—it's about setting up your environment in a way that makes those habits less likely to happen.

Ready to make your bad habits harder to stick with? Let's get started!

Make Bad Habits Hard to Do

Just like you can make good habits easy to start, you can make bad habits harder to do. If you want to stop doing something, like spending too much time playing video games or eating too many snacks, the trick is to put obstacles in your way. This makes the bad habit less tempting.

For example, if you find yourself reaching for your phone when you're supposed to be studying, try putting your phone in another room or giving it to a parent while you work. If you want to eat less junk food, keep snacks out of sight or ask your family to store them in a place that's harder to reach.

By making bad habits harder to do, you'll be less likely to fall back into them. You don't have to rely on willpower alone—just make the bad habits more inconvenient, and you'll find yourself doing them less and less

Create a "Bad Habit Barrier"! If there's a habit you want to break, like watching too much TV, set up a barrier like putting the remote in a drawer across the room. The farther away it is, the less likely you'll be to grab it!

Replace Bad Habits with Good Ones

One of the best ways to stop a bad habit is by replacing it with a good one. Instead of just trying to quit something cold turkey, fill the space with a positive habit that you actually enjoy. This way, you're not just stopping a bad habit—you're swapping it out for something better.

For example, if you tend to watch too much TV, try replacing that time with something more fun or productive, like learning a new skill, playing a sport, or reading a book. If you find yourself snacking when you're bored, try drinking water or going for a quick walk instead.

Replacing a bad habit with a good one makes the transition easier because you're not just telling yourself "no" all the time. Instead, you're giving yourself a new, positive way to spend your time, which feels better and helps you reach your goals

FUN TIP

Turn your replacement habit into a game! For example, if you're trying to stop biting your nails, every time you feel the urge, do 5 jumping jacks instead. Make it fun and challenge yourself to beat your last score each day!

Change Your Environment to Support Good Habits

One powerful way to help good habits stick is to change your environment to support them. Your environment is everything around you—your room, your school, even the people you spend time with. When you change your environment, you make it easier to build good habits and harder to slip into bad ones.

For example, if you want to study more, set up a study space where you won't be distracted. Keep your books, notebook, and pencils right on your desk so everything you need is easy to find. If you want to practice playing an instrument, leave your guitar or piano out in a visible place so you'll be reminded to play.

On the other hand, if you want to stop a bad habit, like playing video games when you should be doing homework, change your environment to remove the temptation. Put your video game controller in a drawer or ask a parent to limit screen time during homework hours.

The key is to make your environment work for you by designing it to support your goals. When your space is set up the right way, it's easier to stay on track

Create a "Habit Zone" in your room! Choose a spot for each good habit—like a reading corner with comfy pillows, a desk for homework, or a sports area with your soccer ball and shoes ready to go. Each time you visit one of your zones, you'll know it's time for that habit!

Ask for Help to Stay on Track

Building new habits can be challenging, but you don't have to do it alone! Asking for help from friends, family, or even teachers can make a big difference. When someone else is encouraging you, it's easier to stay motivated and stick to your habits, especially when you feel like giving up.

You can ask a parent to remind you about your habit, like making sure you practice your piano or finish your homework on time. You can even ask a friend to join you in building a new habit, like going for a run together after school or reading the same book. Having someone to cheer you on makes the habit feel more fun and less like work.

It's also okay to ask for advice if you're struggling to stick with your habit. People who have already built good habits might have tips and tricks to share that can help you succeed

Turn your habit into a team game! Ask a friend or family member to do the habit with you and track your progress together. See who can keep up the habit for the most days in a row, and celebrate each other's wins with small rewards

Use Positive Reminders to Stay Motivated

Sometimes, even with the best intentions, it's easy to forget about your habits. That's where positive reminders come in! A reminder can be something simple, like a note on your desk or a phone alarm, that nudges you to do your habit. And when the reminder is positive and encouraging, it helps you feel excited about completing your habit.

For example, if you're trying to remember to drink more water, you could put a sticky note on the fridge that says, "Drink up—you're doing great!" Or, if you want to read more, leave a note by your bed that says, "Time to dive into your next adventure!" These reminders not only help you stay on track but also give you a little boost of motivation.

You can even set reminders on your phone that pop up at certain times, like after school or before bed, to gently push you toward completing your habit

Create colorful sticky notes with encouraging messages for your habits! Use fun colors and doodles to make each note stand out, like "You've got this!" or "Just one more chapter!" Stick them in places where you'll see them, like your desk, mirror, or book

Chapter #5
Why Habits Are Powerful

Habits might seem like small, everyday actions, but they have the power to shape your entire life. From the moment you wake up to the time you go to bed, many of the things you do are the result of habits. That's because habits are automatic—they save you time and energy by helping you repeat behaviors without having to think too much. And when you build good habits, they help you achieve your goals, become more successful, and feel proud of yourself.

Think about it: If you have the habit of doing your homework every day after school, it helps you stay on top of your work without stress. If you make it a habit to practice a sport or a musical instrument regularly, you'll see yourself getting better over time. Habits may start small, but they add up quickly and can have a huge impact on your life.

The best part is that habits can work for you or against you. If you focus on building good habits, you can achieve amazing things without even realizing it. On the other hand, bad habits can make things harder, so learning how to replace them with better ones is important.

In this chapter, we'll explore why habits are so powerful and how they can help you reach your biggest goals. By understanding the true power of habits, you'll be able to make choices that lead to success and happiness, one small action at a time. Let's dive into how habits can change your life!

Good Habits Save Time

Did you know that having good habits can actually help you save time? When you build habits, you do things automatically without needing to think about them.

This means you can finish tasks faster and free up more time for fun stuff! For example, if you make it a habit to do your homework right after school, you won't have to spend time deciding when to do it—it'll just become part of your routine.

Good habits help you get things done quickly and easily, so you can spend less time worrying about tasks and more time doing the things you enjoy.

Make a list of the things you do every day and see if you can turn them into habits! Once you've created a habit, notice how much time you save and reward yourself with something fun!

Habits Help You Reach Big Goals

Big goals, like getting good grades, learning to play an instrument, or becoming a better athlete, can sometimes feel overwhelming.

But here's the secret: good habits make big goals much easier to achieve! By doing small things every day, like practicing for 10 minutes or reviewing your notes after school, you're taking tiny steps that add up over time.

Instead of focusing on how far away your goal seems, focus on the small daily habits that will help you get there. Before you know it, all those little actions will have brought you closer to reaching your big dreams!

FUN TIP

Set a big goal for yourself and break it into smaller habits. For example, if your goal is to run a mile, start by running for 5 minutes each day. Create a "Goal Tracker" where you check off each day you complete a small habit, and watch how you get closer to your big goal!

BIG GOAL!

- Practice
- Thinking
- Study
- Meditate
- Exercise!

Habits Build Confidence

When you stick to good habits, you start to see yourself getting better at things, and that builds your confidence!

Whether it's studying regularly and seeing your grades improve, practicing a sport and getting stronger, or reading every night and finishing more books, every small habit you complete makes you feel proud of yourself.

The more you follow through on your habits, the more confident you become in your ability to reach your goals.

Good habits show you that you can make progress, even when things seem hard at first.

Each time you achieve a small goal, you build the belief that you can tackle bigger challenges in the future.

Create a "Confidence Wall" where you write down or draw all the things you've accomplished by sticking to your habits. Each time you hit a goal, add it to your wall and watch your confidence grow!

Good Habits Give You Freedom

It might seem like habits are just about sticking to rules or routines, but the truth is, good habits give you freedom! When you make something a habit, like doing your homework right after school or practicing an instrument every day, you get things done more quickly and efficiently.

This leaves you with more free time to do the things you love—like playing games, hanging out with friends, or exploring new hobbies.

Instead of feeling stressed or rushed to finish tasks at the last minute, good habits help you stay organized and in control of your time.

The more you stick to your habits, the more freedom you'll have to enjoy life without worrying about unfinished work.

FUN TIP

Create a "Free Time Jar"! Each time you complete a habit, like finishing homework or practicing, drop a note in the jar. At the end of the week, count how many notes you've collected and reward yourself with fun free-time activities!

Bad Habits Can Sneak Up on You

Bad habits don't always start out as a big deal, but they can sneak up on you before you even realize it!

Sometimes, things that seem harmless—like playing video games for "just a few more minutes" or putting off your homework—can slowly turn into bad habits.

Before you know it, those small actions start to build up, making it harder to focus on what's really important.

Bad habits can be tricky because they often feel easy or fun in the moment, but over time, they can cause stress and make life harder.

The key is to recognize bad habits early and take steps to stop them before they grow into bigger problems.

Play "Habit Detective"! Take a week to track your habits and write down which ones are helpful and which ones might be sneaking up on you. Once you spot a bad habit, write down one action you can take to change it!

Chapter #6
How to Break Bad Habits

We all have bad habits—those little things we do that we know aren't great for us, like procrastinating, spending too much time on screens, or snacking when we're not hungry. The good news is that bad habits don't have to stick around forever. With the right strategies, you can break bad habits and replace them with better ones.

Bad habits often stick because they're easy and tempting. They give us a quick reward, like watching funny videos when we should be studying, or reaching for a snack instead of a healthy meal. But breaking a bad habit doesn't mean you have to rely on willpower alone. There are simple ways to make bad habits harder to do and less attractive.

In this chapter, we'll look at some fun and practical ways to break bad habits. You'll learn how to replace bad habits with good ones, how to remove the things that trigger them, and how to create a plan to avoid falling back into them. By understanding how bad habits work, you'll be able to take control and make changes that help you become the best version of yourself.

Ready to kick those bad habits to the curb? Let's get started!

Make Bad Habits Uncomfortable

One way to stop bad habits is to make them uncomfortable or harder to do. Bad habits often stick because they're easy or fun in the moment, like watching TV when you should be studying.

But if you make it difficult to keep doing the habit, you'll be less likely to fall into the same pattern.

For example, if you spend too much time on your phone, try putting it in another room while you're working. Or if you snack too much, keep unhealthy snacks out of sight.

When bad habits become inconvenient, you're more likely to break them. The more uncomfortable you make them, the less tempting they'll be!

FUN TIP

Create "Habit Obstacles"! For each bad habit you want to break, think of one obstacle you can put in place to make it harder to do. For example, put your video game controller in a drawer while you study or place your phone in a different room during homework time.

Replace Temptations

One of the best ways to break a bad habit is to replace the temptation with something better. Instead of just stopping the bad habit, swap it for a healthier or more productive option.

For example, if you're tempted to snack on chips, replace them with fruits or nuts. If you spend too much time on your phone, swap it for a book or an outdoor activity.

This way, you still satisfy the urge but in a way that benefits you.

Having a better option ready when temptation strikes makes it easier to choose the right action without thinking too much.

The more you replace bad temptations with good ones, the easier it becomes to stick to positive habits.

FUN TIP

Make a "Temptation Swap List"! Write down your bad habits and the things that tempt you. Next to each, write a better option to choose instead, like grabbing a healthy snack or doing something active. Keep the list where you'll see it every day!

Find What Causes Bad Habits

Every bad habit has a cause, something that triggers it and makes you want to do it. Maybe you reach for snacks when you're bored, or you procrastinate when you're stressed.

Understanding what causes your bad habits is the first step toward breaking them. Once you know what triggers the habit, you can take action to avoid it or change how you respond.

For example, if you notice that you tend to watch too much TV when you're feeling tired after school, you can plan a different activity, like going for a walk or listening to music, to break the habit. Or, if you snack when you're bored, you can replace that with something else, like reading or playing a game. By identifying the cause, you take control of your actions and can change the way you respond.

FUN TIP

Be a "Habit Detective"! Spend a few days tracking your habits and figure out what causes them. Once you've spotted the triggers, write down a new action you can take instead, like drinking water when you crave snacks or taking a break when you feel tired.

Change the Cue

A cue is what triggers your habit—it's the thing that reminds you to start it.

For example, if you always check your phone when you see it next to your bed, the phone is the cue for that habit. If you want to break a bad habit, one of the best things you can do is change the cue. By removing or changing the thing that triggers the habit, you can make it much easier to stop.

For instance, if you tend to snack every time you see a bag of chips in the kitchen, you can change the cue by moving the snacks out of sight. Or if your phone distracts you from studying, keep it in another room while you work. When you change the cue, the temptation to do the bad habit gets smaller, and it becomes easier to stay focused on your goals.

FUN TIP

Do a "Cue Makeover"! Look around your room and see if there are any cues that trigger bad habits. Rearrange your space or remove items that might be causing those habits, like moving your phone away from your desk during homework time or putting unhealthy snacks in a less accessible spot.

Change the Cue

A cue is what triggers your habit—it's the thing that reminds you to start it.

For example, if you always check your phone when you see it next to your bed, the phone is the cue for that habit. If you want to break a bad habit, one of the best things you can do is change the cue. By removing or changing the thing that triggers the habit, you can make it much easier to stop.

For instance, if you tend to snack every time you see a bag of chips in the kitchen, you can change the cue by moving the snacks out of sight. Or if your phone distracts you from studying, keep it in another room while you work. When you change the cue, the temptation to do the bad habit gets smaller, and it becomes easier to stay focused on your goals.

Do a "Cue Makeover"! Look around your room and see if there are any cues that trigger bad habits. Rearrange your space or remove items that might be causing those habits, like moving your phone away from your desk during homework time or putting unhealthy snacks in a less accessible spot.

Get Support from Friends or Family

Breaking bad habits or building new ones can be a lot easier when you have support from your friends or family. Sometimes, having someone remind you to stay on track or encourage you when things get tough is just what you need to keep going.

Whether it's asking a friend to join you in a new habit, or getting a family member to remind you to avoid a bad habit, having someone by your side makes the process more fun and easier to stick with.

For example, if you're trying to break the habit of procrastinating, you could ask a parent or sibling to check in and see if you've finished your homework on time. Or if you're trying to build a habit of exercising more, invite a friend to go for a walk or play outside with you. Working on habits together makes it more enjoyable, and you can celebrate your successes along the way!

FUN TIP

Create a "Habit Buddy Pact"! Ask a friend or family member to be your habit buddy, and write down your goals together. Help each other stick to your habits by checking in regularly, and celebrate when you both reach a milestone.

Chapter #7
Keeping Up with Good Habits

Building good habits is a great first step, but the real challenge is keeping them up over time. It's easy to feel excited when you start a new habit, like practicing a sport, reading more, or staying organized. But what happens when the excitement fades or when you have a busy day? That's when it's most important to stick to your habits.

The secret to keeping up with good habits is making them a natural part of your daily routine, like brushing your teeth or getting dressed. When a habit becomes automatic, you don't have to think about it anymore—you just do it! And even if you miss a day here and there, it's important to jump right back in so you don't lose the progress you've made.

In this chapter, we'll explore ways to stay consistent with your good habits. You'll learn how to stay motivated, track your progress, and find fun ways to reward yourself for sticking to your goals. Keeping up with good habits doesn't have to be hard—with the right tools, it can become something you look forward to every day.

Ready to make your good habits last? Let's dive in and learn how to stay on track!

Track Your Progress to See How Far You've Come

Tracking your progress is one of the best ways to stay motivated when building a habit. When you can see how many days you've kept up with your habit, it's easier to keep going and not give up. Plus, it feels really rewarding to see all the effort you've put in!

You can use a calendar, habit tracker, or even just a piece of paper to mark each day you complete your habit. For example, if you want to practice the guitar every day, mark an "X" on your calendar each time you practice. Over time, you'll have a long chain of "X"s, and you won't want to break the streak!

By tracking your progress, you also see how small, consistent actions add up over time. Even if you don't notice huge changes at first, every day that you stick to your habit is a step toward reaching your goal

FUN TIP

Turn your habit tracker into a "Habit Rainbow"! For every day you complete your habit, color in a stripe of the rainbow. By the end of the week, you'll have a colorful reminder of how far you've come!

Don't Miss Two Days in a Row

It's okay if you miss a day in your habit—life happens! But here's a great rule to follow: never miss two days in a row. Missing one day won't stop your progress, but missing two days makes it easier to fall out of your habit completely. The trick is to get back on track quickly and keep your habit streak going.

For example, if you miss a day of doing your homework right after school, don't worry too much. Just make sure to do it the next day. The key is not letting one missed day turn into a missed week. Remember, the goal isn't to be perfect, but to stay consistent.

By following the "don't miss two days" rule, you're giving yourself the freedom to make mistakes while still staying committed to your habit.

FUN TIP

Create a "Bounce Back Plan"! Write down what you'll do if you miss a day of your habit, like setting an extra reminder or asking a friend to help. That way, you'll have a plan in place to get back on track quickly.

Focus on the Long Term

Building good habits isn't about seeing results right away—it's about the progress you make over time. Sometimes, you might not notice the benefits of your habit right away, and that can be frustrating. But the real power of habits comes from doing them consistently over weeks, months, and even years. That's when the big changes start to happen.

Think of it like planting a tree. At first, all you see is a tiny sprout, but with water and care every day, it eventually grows into a tall, strong tree. Your habits work the same way! Whether it's learning a new skill, becoming better at a sport, or getting good grades, your daily habits are like watering that tree. It takes time, but the results will come.

When you focus on the long-term benefits, it's easier to stay motivated, even when you don't see changes right away. Every small action adds up, and by sticking with your habits, you're setting yourself up for success in the future

FUN TIP

Make a "Future Vision Board"! Grab some old magazines or print pictures that represent your goals—like a basketball if you're working on your game or books if you want to improve your grades. Glue these onto a board or paper and keep it in your room. Every time you see it, you'll remember that your habits are helping you reach those big, long-term dreams

Find a Habit Buddy

Doing things together is always more fun, and the same goes for building habits. Finding a friend or family member to be your habit buddy can make the process much easier and more exciting. When you have someone to share your progress with or do activities together, it's easier to stay motivated and stick to your goals.

For example, if you and a friend both want to get better at running, you could agree to run together a few times a week. Or, if you want to read more, you can choose a book with a sibling or classmate and read it at the same time. A habit buddy can also remind you to stay on track when you feel like skipping a day.

Having someone to celebrate small wins with makes the journey more enjoyable. Plus, you can help keep each other accountable and cheer each other on!

FUN TIP

Create a "Habit Buddy Pact"! Write down your goals and agree on how you'll support each other. Maybe it's a quick text to remind each other or a celebration when you both reach your milestones. Keep the pact in a special place to remind you of your commitment!

Build Routines

A great way to make your habits stick is by turning them into part of a daily routine. A routine is a set of habits you do in the same order, at the same time, every day. Routines make habits easier because your brain doesn't have to think about what to do next—it's already planned out!

For example, you could create a morning routine that starts with brushing your teeth, then eating breakfast, and then reading for 10 minutes. Or you could have a bedtime routine that includes putting your things away, taking a shower, and doing a quick review of your homework for the next day. When habits are part of a routine, they become automatic, and you're more likely to stick to them.

By building routines, you're making sure that good habits happen every day, without having to rely on willpower or remembering to do them. It's like setting up your day for success!

Create a "Routine Checklist"! Write down your morning, after-school, or bedtime routine and put it somewhere you'll see it, like your bedroom door or bathroom mirror. Each time you complete a task, check it off—it feels great to see all those checkmarks!

Daily Routine

Chapter #7
How to Make Habits Fun

Let's face it: some habits can feel like chores. Whether it's doing homework, practicing an instrument, or cleaning your room, sticking to a habit can sometimes seem boring. But here's a secret: habits don't have to feel like work—you can make them fun! When you enjoy what you're doing, you're much more likely to keep it up and even look forward to it.

Making a habit fun means finding ways to turn it into something you enjoy. Love music? Play your favorite songs while you clean your room. Like a challenge? Turn studying into a game where you race against the clock. The more you personalize your habits to make them fun and rewarding, the easier it becomes to stick with them.

In this chapter, you'll learn creative and exciting ways to make your habits more fun. Whether it's adding rewards, turning it into a competition, or making it a team effort with friends, you'll discover how to make even the most boring habits feel enjoyable. By adding a little fun to your routine, you'll be surprised at how much easier it is to reach your goals.

Ready to have fun while building great habits? Let's jump in and explore how to make habit-building a blast!

Make Habits Fun

One of the best ways to keep up with a habit is to make it fun! If a habit feels like a boring chore, it's easy to lose interest. But when you find ways to enjoy the process, you'll look forward to doing it every day.

For example, if you want to build a habit of cleaning your room, you could play your favorite music while you clean. If you're trying to exercise more, turn it into a game by challenging yourself to see how many jumping jacks or push-ups you can do in one minute. The more you can turn your habits into something fun, the easier it will be to stick with them.

Adding a fun twist to your habits can also help you stay motivated on days when you don't feel like doing them. When you make your habit something you enjoy, it feels less like work and more like a reward in itself

Turn your habit into a game! For example, if you're reading, challenge yourself to see how many pages you can finish in 10 minutes. If you're practicing an instrument, make up a fun song or rhythm. You can even create a "Habit Scoreboard" to track your progress and give yourself points for completing your habit each day!

Reward Yourself

One of the best ways to keep a habit going is to reward yourself after you complete it.

Rewards make habits more fun and give you something to look forward to.

For example, if you finish your homework on time, treat yourself by watching your favorite TV show or playing a game for a bit. These small rewards help your brain associate the habit with something positive, which makes you want to do it again!

Rewards don't have to be big—they can be simple things you enjoy, like having a snack, reading a book, or taking a break to do something fun. By rewarding yourself after you finish a habit, you're more likely to stick with it and feel good about the progress you're making

FUN TIP

Create a "Reward Box"! Write down fun rewards, like "Play a video game," "Watch a movie," or "Eat a treat," on slips of paper and put them in a box. Each time you complete your habit, pull a reward from the box and enjoy it!

Visualize Success

A powerful way to stay motivated with your habits is to visualize your success. This means taking a moment to imagine how great you'll feel after sticking to your habit.

For example, if you're building an exercise habit, picture how much stronger and healthier you'll be after exercising every day. Or, if you're working on studying more, imagine how proud you'll feel when you see your grades improve.

When you visualize your success, you give yourself a clear picture of what you're working toward. It helps keep you focused on the positive results of your habit, even when it feels hard to stick with it.

The more you can see the future benefits in your mind, the easier it becomes to stay motivated in the present

FUN TIP

Make a "Success Poster"! Draw or print pictures of what you want to achieve with your habit, like being stronger, getting better grades, or mastering a skill. Hang the poster where you can see it every day to remind yourself of how great it will feel when you reach your goal

Compete with Yourself

A fun way to stay motivated with your habits is to compete with yourself! Set a small goal, like running for 5 minutes, and then try to beat that record the next time by going for 6 minutes.

This turns your habit into a personal challenge, where you're always trying to do a little bit better than before. Whether it's reading more pages, doing more push-ups, or studying for an extra 5 minutes, competing with yourself makes building habits exciting and helps you keep improving.

By trying to beat your own best, you can make steady progress while having fun. It feels great to see yourself get better each day, and the more you push yourself, the more satisfying the rewards will be!

FUN TIP

Create a "Personal Best" chart! Each time you break your own record for a habit—like running longer or reading more—write it down on your chart. See how many personal bests you can collect over time!

Mix It Up

If a habit starts to feel boring, the best way to keep it going is to mix it up! Doing the same thing every day can get repetitive, so changing how you do your habit can make it more exciting.

For example, if you usually run outside, try running in a new park or even on a treadmill. If you usually study in your room, try studying at the library or outside in the backyard. These small changes can make your habit feel fresh and fun again.

By adding variety, you can avoid getting stuck in a routine that feels dull. Mixing things up keeps your habit interesting and helps you stay motivated to stick with it.

The key is to be creative and make little tweaks to your routine so it always feels new and exciting!

FUN TIP

Create a "Habit Adventure List"! Write down different ways you can mix up your habit. For example, if you love reading, list new places to read, like the park, a cozy corner, or even outside under a tree. Each time you try a new spot or method, check it off the list!

Your Habit-Building Journey Begins Now!

Congratulations! You've made it to the end of the book, but this is really just the beginning of your habit-building journey. You've learned how habits work, how to create new ones, how to break bad ones, and most importantly, how to make habits fun and rewarding.

Now it's time to take everything you've learned and put it into action! Start small, be patient with yourself, and remember that every tiny step counts. Whether you want to get better at school, improve at a sport, or simply stay organized, building good habits will help you achieve your goals.

Along the way, don't forget to celebrate your progress, reward yourself for sticking with it, and mix things up when you need to keep it exciting. Habits are the building blocks of success, and now you have the tools to create habits that help you become the best version of yourself.

Remember, no one's perfect, and it's okay to slip up sometimes. What matters most is that you keep going and never give up on your goals. Each day is a new chance to build the habits that will shape your future. Good luck, and keep building those amazing habits! Your future self will thank you!